21355 Intermediate Piano Solo

$2.50 in USA

Canterbury Bells

Judy East Wells

intermediate

Alfred
THE ALFRED SIGNATURE SERIES

for Graysen

Canterbury Bells

Judy East Wells

ISBN 0-7390-2991-6

17
RH
LH 5
over
21
f
25
8va
29
33
mf
mp

9780739029916
TP
APEX

Alfred Publishing Co., Inc.
16320 Roscoe Blvd., Suite 100 • P.O. Box 10003 • Van Nuys,
www.alfred.com